Celtic Guitar

GLENN WEISER

Alfred Music
P.O. Box 10003
Van Nuys, CA 91410-0003
alfred.com

ISBN-10: 0-7692-9680-7 (Book & CD)
ISBN-13: 978-0-7692-9680-7 (Book & CD)

Cover guitar photo courtesy Daisy Rock Guitars.

Introduction

Even though the guitar is not a traditional Celtic instrument, few things sound as sweet as a good arrangement of an Irish or Scottish tune played on acoustic guitar.

This is a collection of 40 traditional Irish and Scottish tunes arranged for fingerstyle guitar, with harmonizing bass lines. These melodies were originally sung or played on fiddle, tinwhistle, bagpipes, or harp and are from a collection of about three hundred traditional tunes that I have arranged over the last 20 years. Two other volumes, *Celtic Harp Music of Carolan and Others for Solo Guitar* and *The Celtic Encyclopedia: Fingerstyle Guitar Edition* are already in print; here I can thank Aaron Stang of Warner Bros. Publications for making these new arrangements available.

The first section of the book consists of airs, laments, pipe tunes, a waltz, and a love song.

Turlough O'Carolan (1670–1738) was an Irish harper who began his career as a traditional musician but became influenced in his many compositions by the Italian Baroque music he heard in the mansions of his wealthy patrons. His music was revived by Irish scholars in the 1950s and was popularized by the Chieftains in the 1970s. Six of Carolan's tunes make up the second part. In 1962, British fingerstyle guitarist Davy Graham devised DADGAD tuning after hearing the music of the oud, a lutelike, fretless stringed instrument, in Tunisia. DADGAD has since become a favorite among Celtic guitarists.

The remaining three sections are dance tunes: reels, jigs, and hornpipes.

To learn more about Celtic guitar, visit my Web site at:
       www.celticguitarmusic.com

Correspondence can also be addressed to me at:
       P.O. Box 2551
       Albany, NY 12220, U.S.A.

May the tunes give you many happy hours.

Glenn Weiser
Albany, 11/99

Contents

CD Index

Airs, Marches & Waltzes

BONNIE DUNDEE

Traditional Scottish
Arr. G. Weiser

This is a 6/8 pipe march. "Bonnie Dundee" was the nickname of the Scottish Jacobite general, James Graham of Claverhouse, who was killed in the Battle of Killiecrankie on July 27, 1689. This arrangement is designed to mimic the sound of the Highland pipes by having the right hand thumb and index finger pinch octaves or fifths in the bass to create the effects of the drones while the middle and ring fingers play an ornamented melody. It was originally published in the August 1998 issue of *Acoustic Guitar*.

jack o'hazeldon

Traditional Scottish
Arr. G. Weiser

This is a beautiful Scottish love song.

0439B

KATIE DWYER

Traditional Irish
Arr. G. Weiser

The name Katie Dwyer was used in eighteenth-century Irish poetry as a sobriquet for Ireland.
This is on the Chieftains' seventh album, and can also be found in *The Roche Collection*.

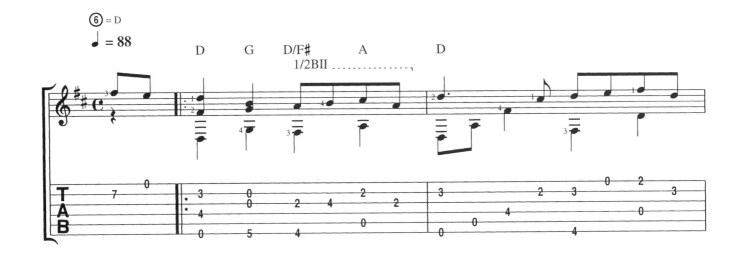

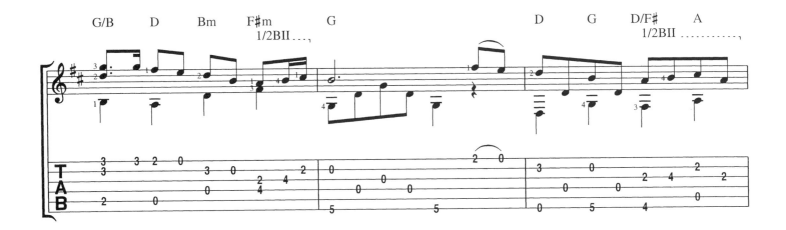

0439B

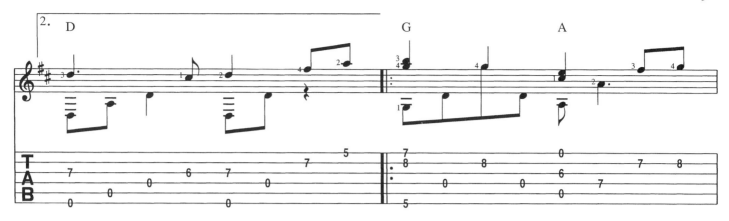

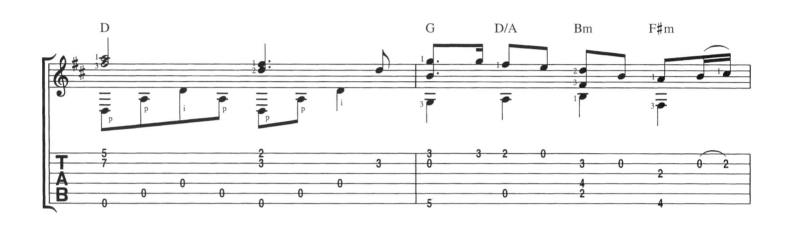

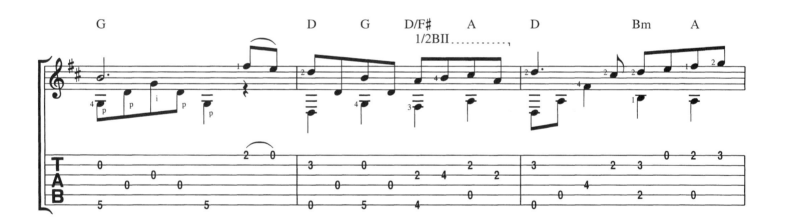

0439B

LORD LOVAT'S LAMENT

Traditional Scottish
Arr. G. Weiser

This is a Highland bagpipe tune which I have worked out for the guitar in two variations. The first part represents a pipe solo in the style of "Bonnie Dundee." When the tune repeats, the thumb shifts to a conventional alternating pattern in order to convey the effect of the entrance of the drum and pipe corps as the full band takes up the melody. I usually play this part faster than the first.

Lord Lovat was the Duke of Atholl and fought for Bonnie Prince Charlie during the Jacobite uprising of 1745 - 1746. After the rebellion was put down, he became the fifth the last person to be beheaded as a traitor on Tower Hill in London.

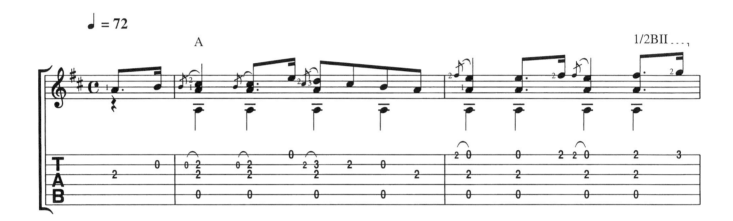

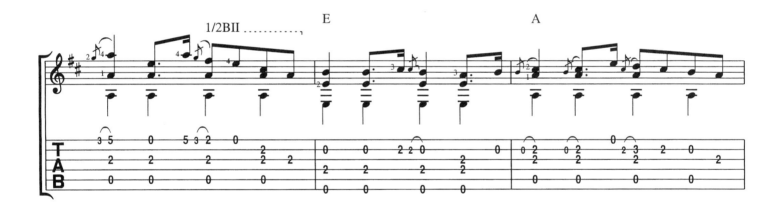

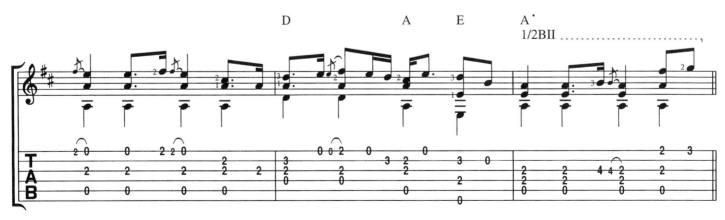

0439B

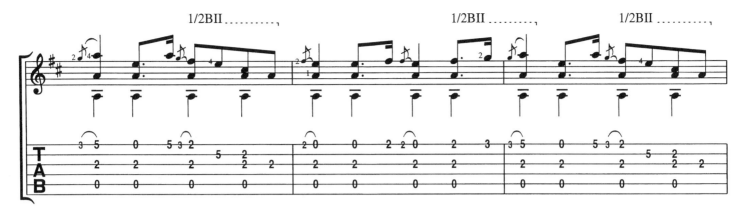

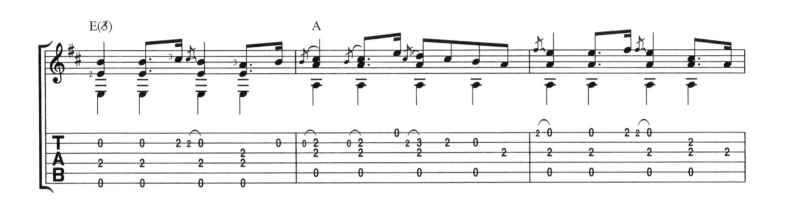

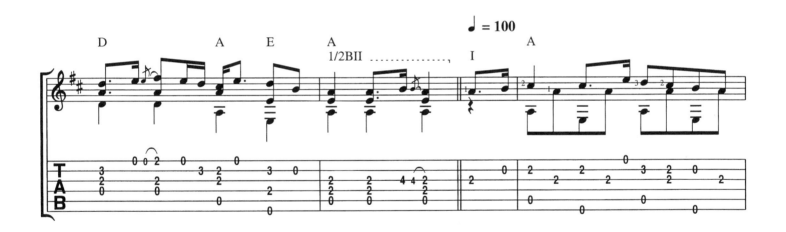

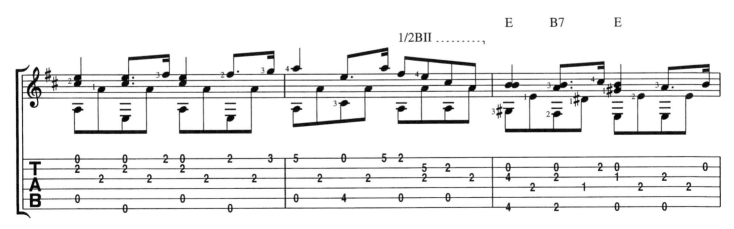

12

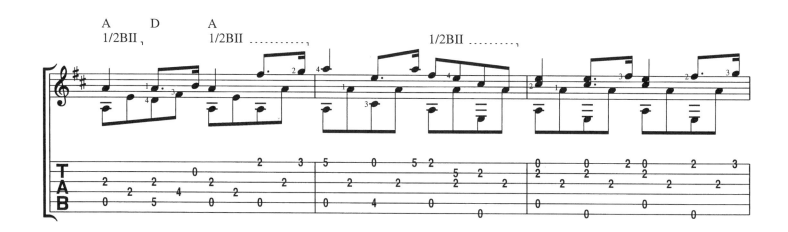

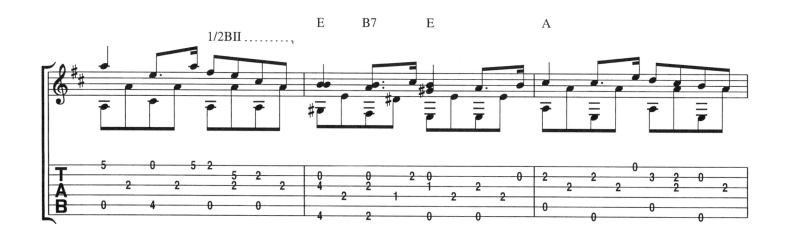

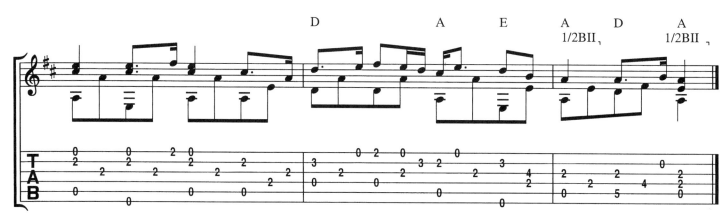

the southwind

Traditional Irish
Arr. G. Weiser

This serene, perfectly titled tune can be found in the *Bunting Collection*.

O'Connell's Lamentation

Traditional Irish
Arr. G. Weiser

This can be found in *O'Neill's Music of Ireland*. It was probably composed as a lament for the great nineteenth-century Irish statesman Daniel O'Connell.

O'Carolan

BLIND MARY

Turlough O'Carolan
Arr. G. Weiser

This tender tune is attributed to Carolan, and is thought to have been composed by him for a blind harper named Maire Dhall. It is considered uncharacteristic of Carolan's style.

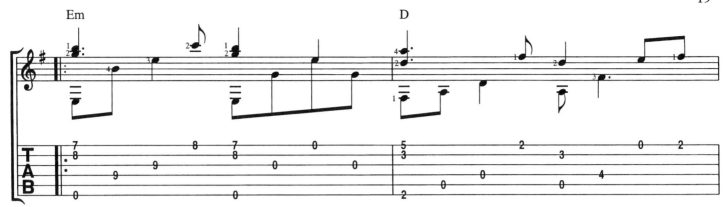

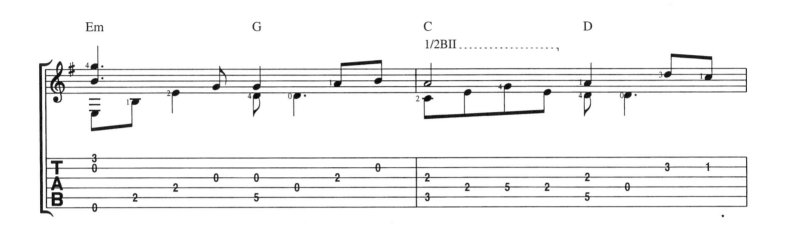

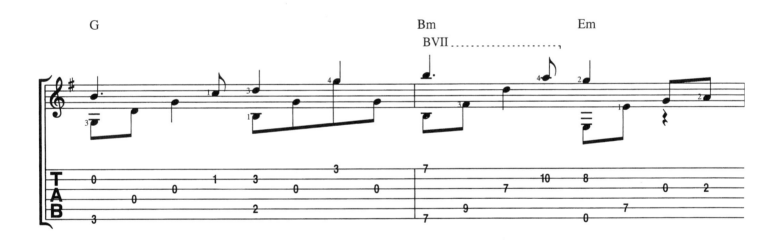

0439B

SIR FESTUS BURKE

Turlough O'Carolan
Arr. G. Weiser

Carolan wrote tunes for several members of this family. Sir Festus was the 5th Baronet of Glinsk in County Galway.

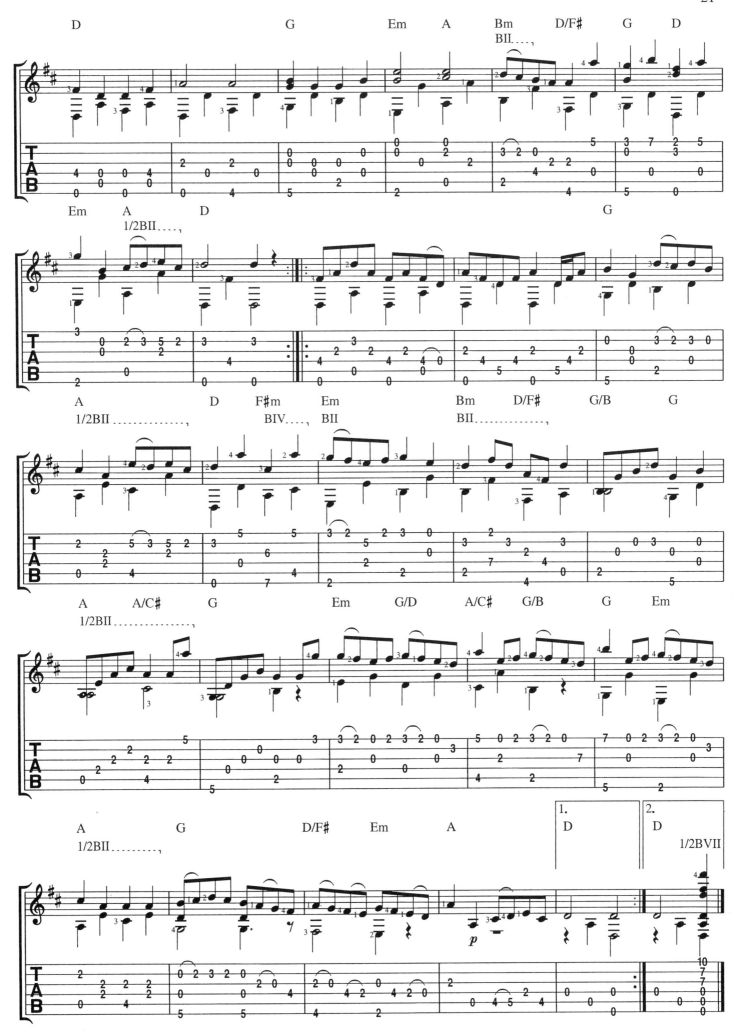

21

0439B

Carolan's Draught

Turlough O'Carolan
Arr. G. Weiser

As the title suggests, Carolan liked a good drink as well as the next man. This tune was collected in the nineteenth-century by Father Walsh of Smeem, about whom the famous song "Father O'Flynn" (or "Top of Cork Road") was written.

CONSTANTINE MAGUIRE

Turlough O'Carolan
Arr. G. Weiser

Constantine Maguire was a colonel who is best known for having arranged an introduction between Carolan and the South Ulster poet Seamus MacCuarta.

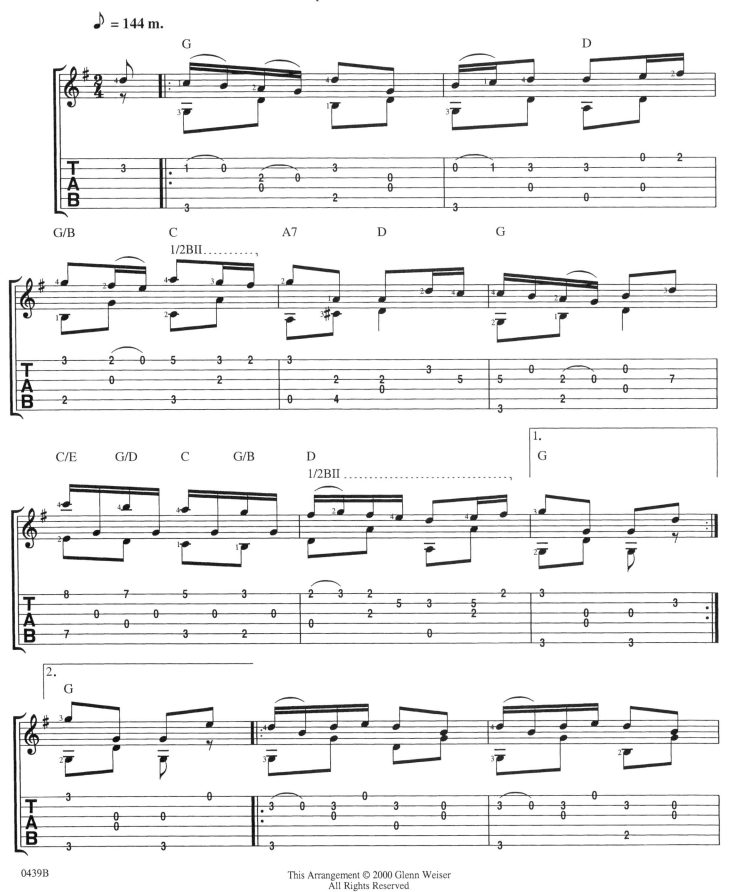

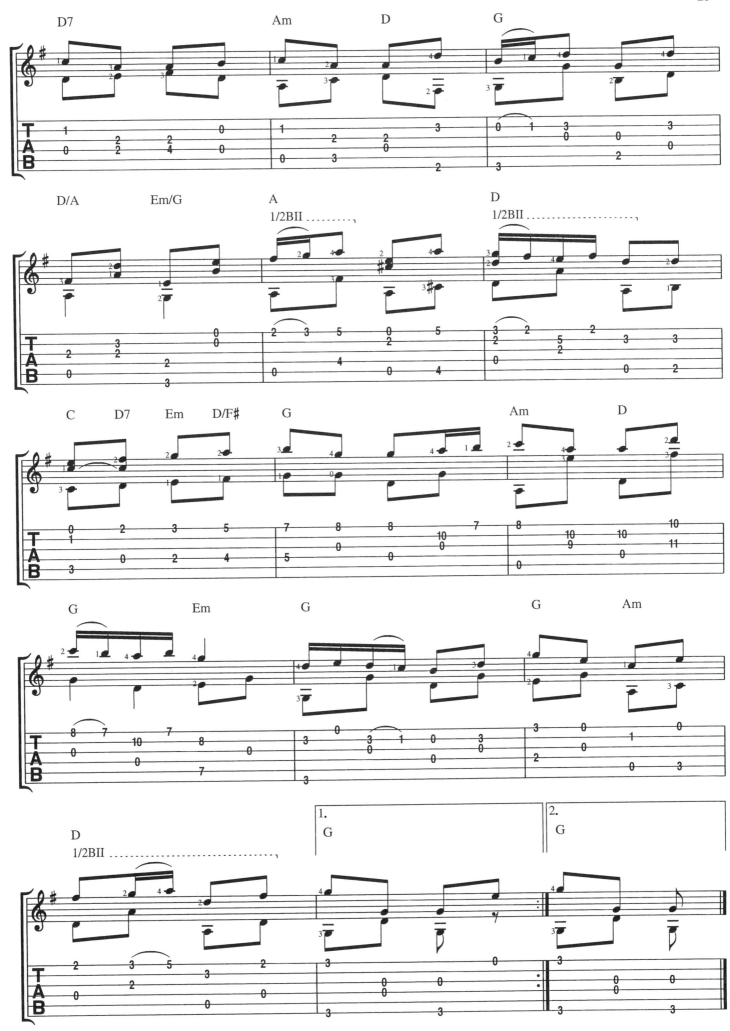

0439B

PLANTXY IRWIN

Turlough O'Carolan
Arr. G. Weiser

This piece was composed for Colonel John Irwin and was originally played as a slow jig. However, the piece is also quite effective as a waltz, and seems to be the quintessential farewell when thus slowed in tempo. It has been worked out in two different octaves, which is a rarity for Celtic guitar arrangements.

0439B

0439B

Charles O'Conor

Turlough O' Carolan
Arr. G. Weiser

Charles O'Conor was a harp student of Carolan's. His diaries are an important source of information about Carolan's life.

Reels

Drowsy Maggie

Traditional Irish
Arr. G. Weiser

This is an E Dorian tune in dropped D tuning. Technically it is a single reel, which is characterized by a four-measure repeating first part and an eight-measure non-repeating second part. Drowsy Maggie's alter ego, "Sleepy Maggie" appears later on.

sleepy maggie

Traditional Irish
Arr. G. Weiser

Despite the similarity in titles, this tune does not seem to be a variant of "Drowsy Maggie." The source for this setting is *Cole's 1000 Fiddle Tunes*. A somewhat different version has been recorded by Eric Schoenberg on his rounder album, *Acoustic Guitar*.

THE GREEN FIELDS OF AMERICA

Traditional Irish
Arr. G. Weiser

This tune can be found in *Cole's 1000 Fiddle Tunes* and appears in *The Roche Collection* under the name of "Molly Brauligan." (By the way, it is quite common for a tune to have more than one name. Brendan Breathnach, in his book *Folk Music and Dances of Ireland*, cites an instance where one tune was found to have sixty different titles, and another instance when one title was applied to six different tunes.)

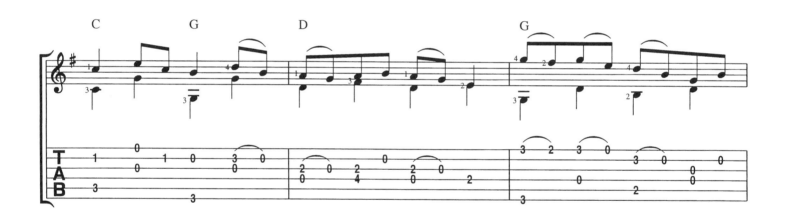

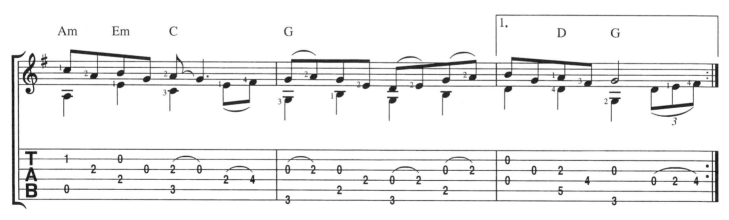

0439B

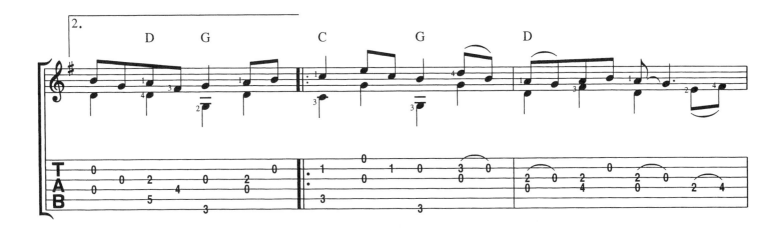

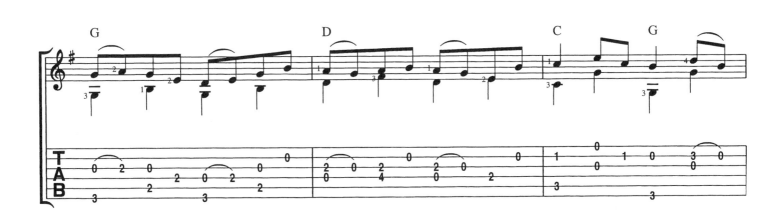

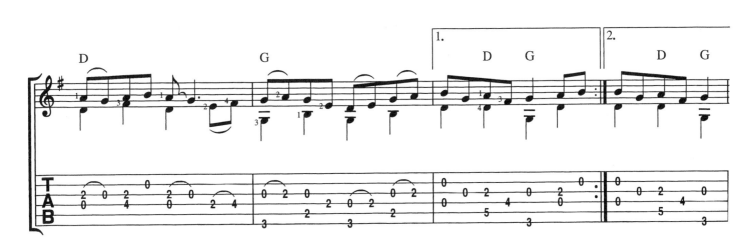

0439B

MAID BEHIND THE BAR

Traditional Irish
Arr. G. Weiser

Also known as "Judy's Reel," this exuberant Irish tune is one my favorites.

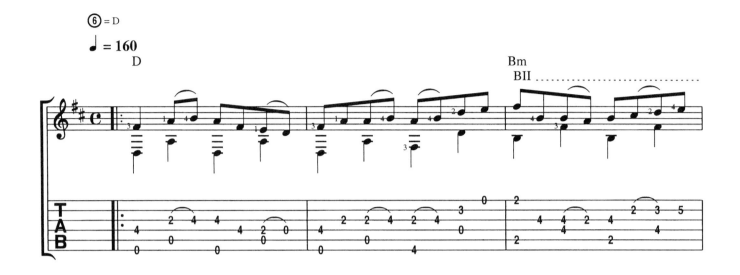

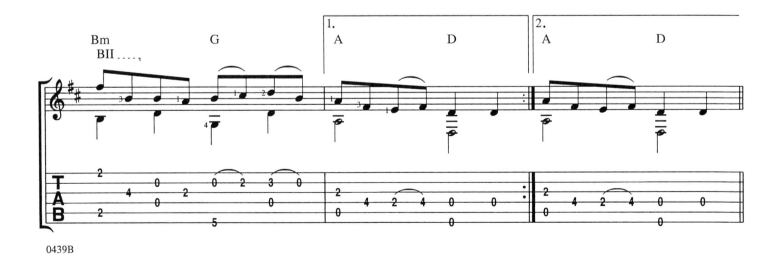

0439B

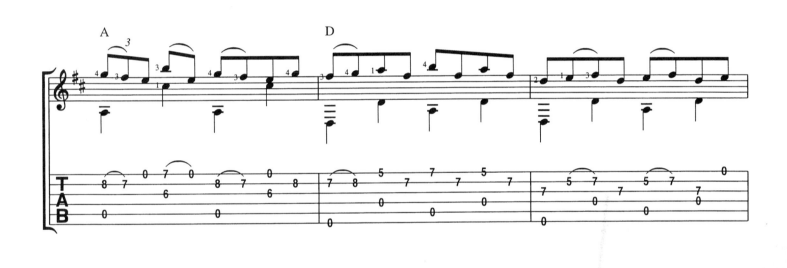

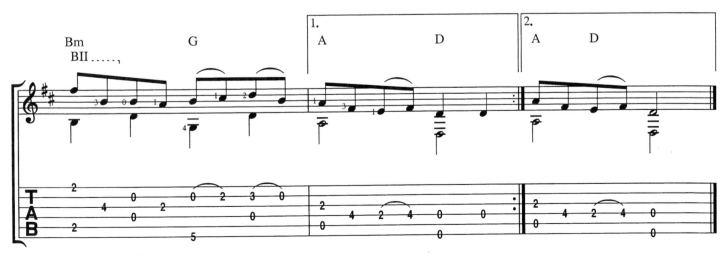

0439B

Napoleon Crossing the Rhine

Traditional Irish
Arr. G. Weiser

This is a stirring Irish reel, formerly known as "Listowell." The Irish commonly named or renamed tunes after Bonaparte, who they hoped would liberate Ireland from the cruel oppression of the English. Unfortunately, the much hoped-for succor from France never arrived.

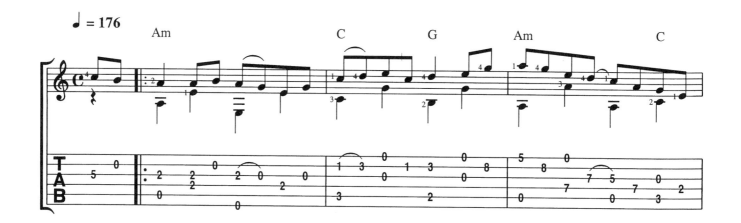

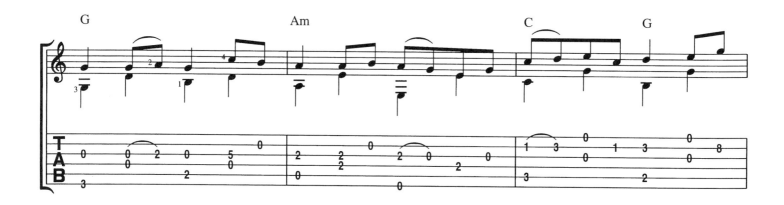

0439B

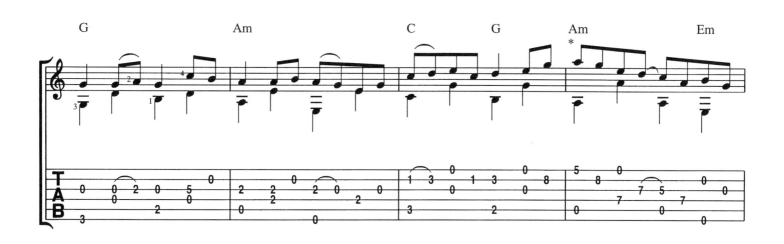

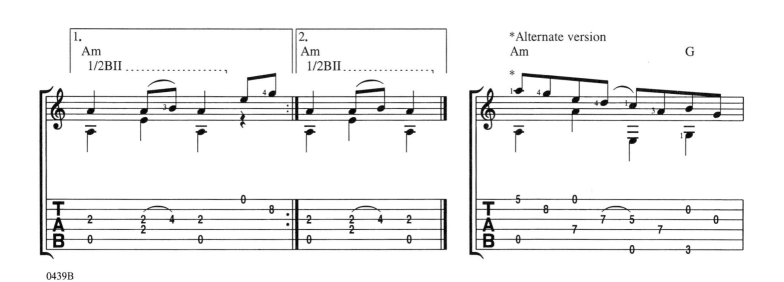

paddy on the railroad

Traditional Irish
Arr. G. Weiser

This tune, which can be found in *Cole's 1000 Fiddle Tunes*, also appears in *O'Neill's Music of Ireland* under the title "The Merry Blacksmith."

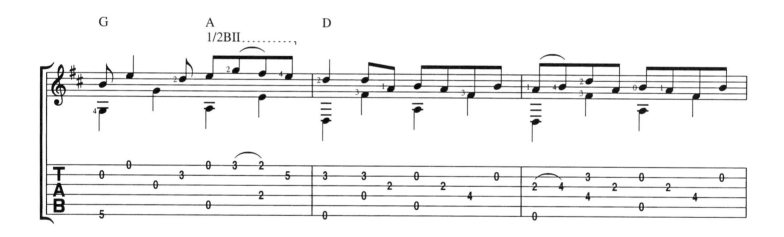

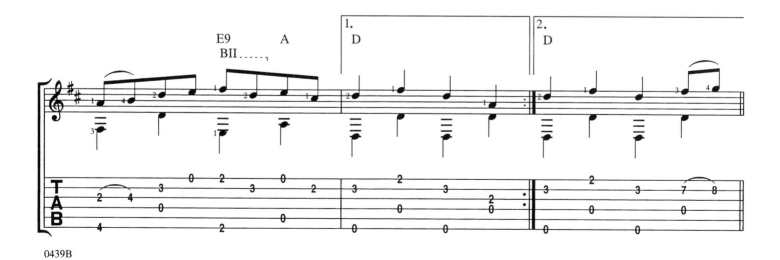

0439B

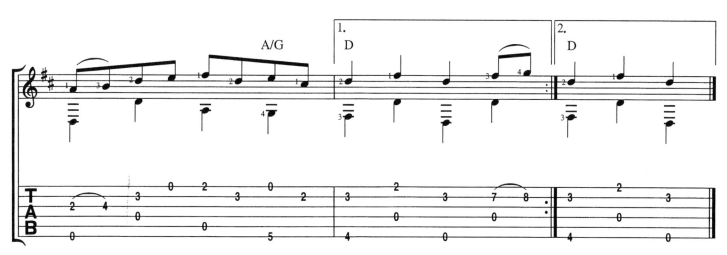

0439B

STATEN ISLANÖ hORNPIPE

Traditional Irish
Arr. G. Weiser

This is an Irish tune that got retitled somewhere along the way and turned from a hornpipe into a reel as well.

THE TEMPERANCE REEL

Traditional Irish
Arr. G. Weiser

Also known as the "Teetotaler's Reel," this tune is a contradance favorite.

0439B

ADGAD

CARRICKFERGUS

Traditional Irish
Arr. G. Weiser

The city of Carrickfergus lies on the East Coast of Ulster in County Antrim not far from Belfast. This song is famous, and has been recorded by Van Morrison with the Chieftans.

farewell to whiskey

Neil Gow
Arr. G. Weiser

This is a strathspey, which is a type of slow reel that became popular in Scotland in the 1700's. This tune was written by Neil Gow, who was a court fiddler for the Duke of Atholl, when the British banned the distillation of spirits. Incidentally, when the English decided to stop being killjoys and let the Scots have their favorite beverage back, Gow wrote another tune entitled "Whiskey Welcome Again." When I visited Blair Atholl in 1997, I saw Neil Gow's fiddle and also was given a private viewing of Gow's famous oil portrait.

0439B

the harvest home

Traditional Irish
Arr. G. Weiser

I learned this Irish hornpipe from Linda Baker, a traditional musician in the Albany, NY area.

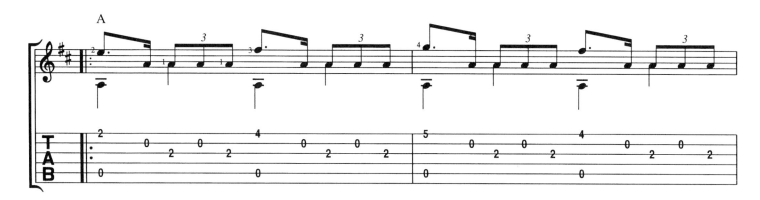

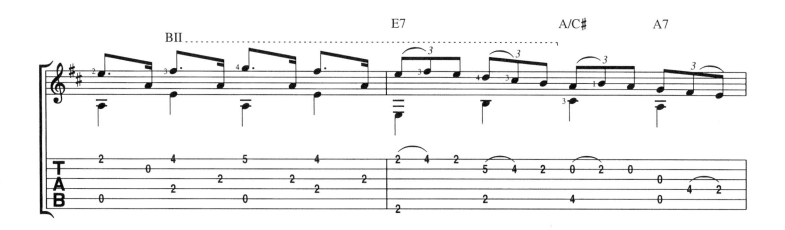

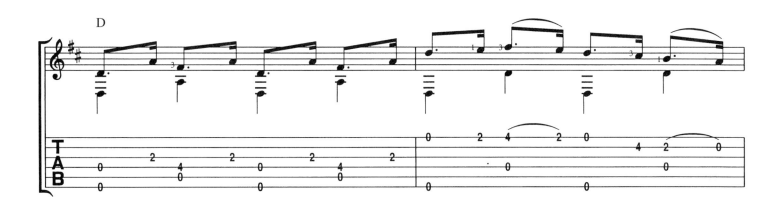

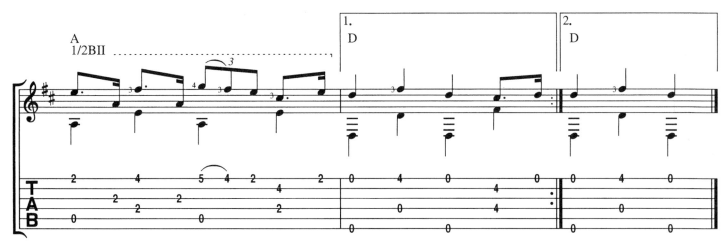

0439B

STAR OF THE COUNTY DOWN

Traditional Irish
Arr. G. Weiser

This is a famous song about a lovestruck young man and the object of his yearning Ulster. This tune also occurs in common-time versions. Incidentally, my mother was born in County Down.

♩ = 108 m.

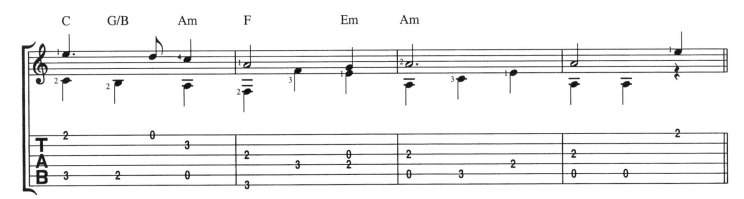

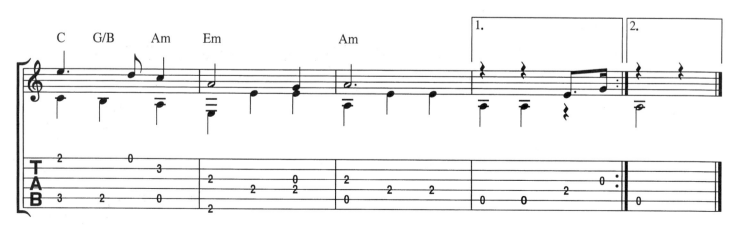

0439B

THE TRAVELER

Traditional Irish
Arr. G. Weiser

Travelers are what the Irish call the Gypsies, who used to roam the countryside in brightly painted horse-drawn wagons and were often tinkers by trade.

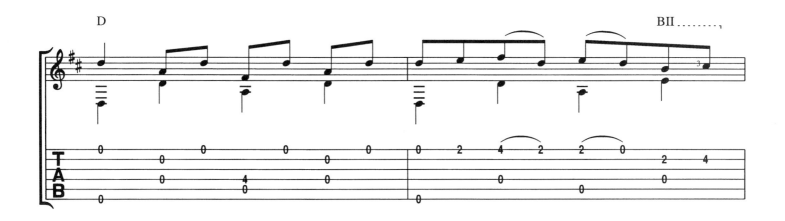

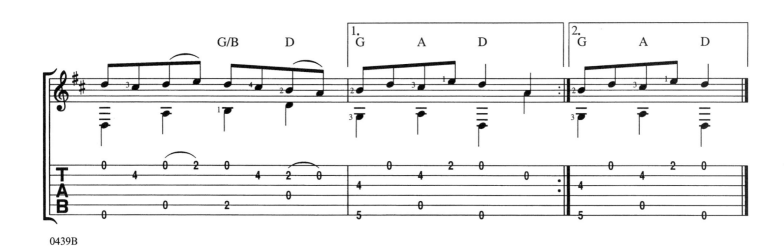

0439B

GARRET BARRY'S JIG

Traditional Irish
Arr. G. Weiser

This Mixolydian tune is named after Garrett Barry, who was a blind Irish minstrel. With this piece, the chief technical consideration is the rhythmic coordination of the numerous hammers and pulls.

Jigs

castle drummond

Traditional Irish
Arr. G. Weiser

I first heard this Scottish jig on a harp record by Allison Kinnaird in a slow version, and then heard Johnny Cunningham fiddle it at quite a brisk pace. This version is based on the slower setting. You can find it in *Kerr's Merry Melodies*.

the hundred pipers

Traditional Irish
Arr. G. Weiser

This Scottish jig can only be described as delightful. When I first heard it, it seemed like I had known the tune forever, so natural and graceful did the melody sound to me. This version comes from the *New England Fiddler's Repertory*. There is even a brand of Scotch named after this tune.

the gallowglass

Traditional Irish
Arr. G. Weiser

I came across this pretty tune in *O'Neill's Music of Ireland,* and made the small alteration of changing all the G sharps to G naturals (natural sevenths in minor mode tunes are more typical of traditional Irish music). In the first part, sixth measure, note the use of the half-barre with the fourth finger on the fifth fret.

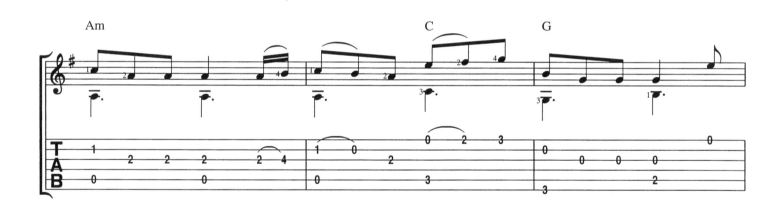

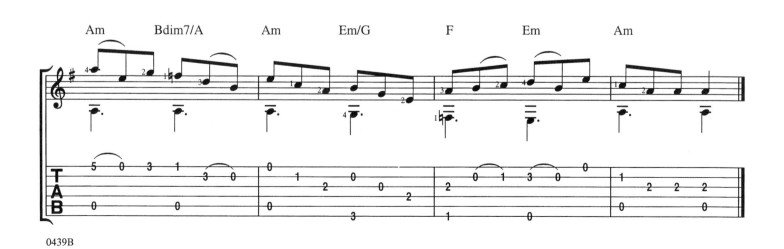

0439B

Langstrom's Pony

Traditional Shetland
Arr. G. Weiser

This four-part Mixolydian tune, like "Gary Owen," is one of those "perpetual" tunes that does not end through the usual process of melodic resolution - therefore an ending has been provided.

0439B

0439B

MORRISON'S JIG

Traditional Irish
Arr. G. Weiser

James Morrison was an Irish fiddler from the Sligo area who made several influential recordings in the 1920's. This jig was probably composed by him.

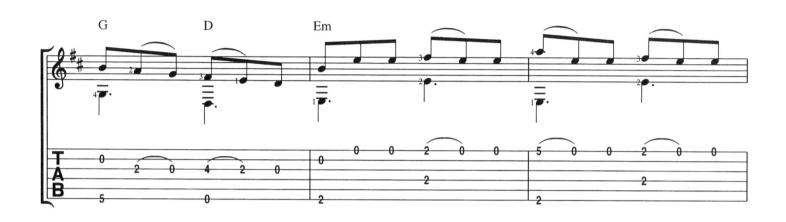

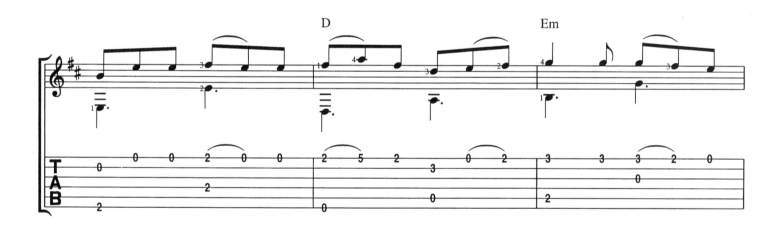

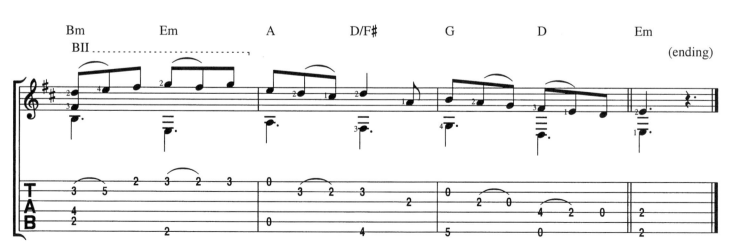

0439B

Top of Cork Road

Traditional Irish
Arr. G. Weiser

This tune, also named "Father O' Flynn" after a nineteenth-century Irish priest who also collected tunes, has the gentle, rolling quality characteristic of so many jigs.

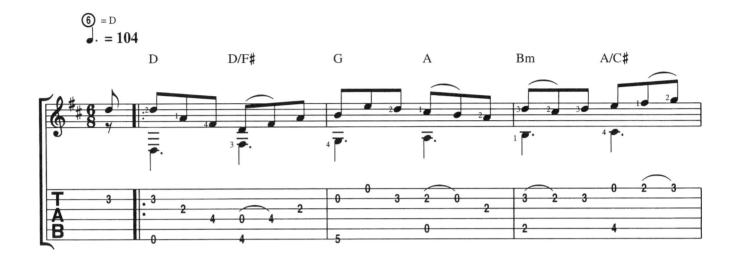

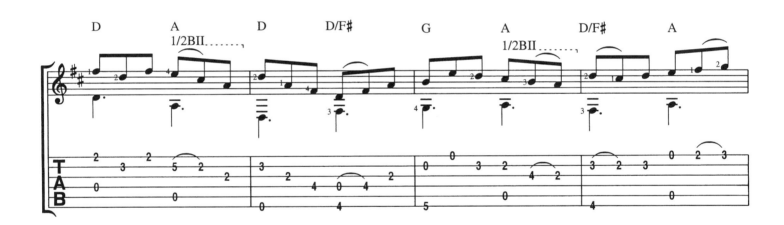

0439B

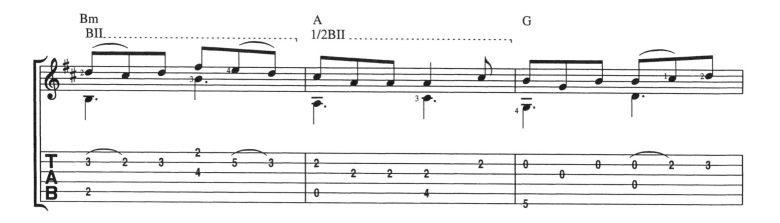

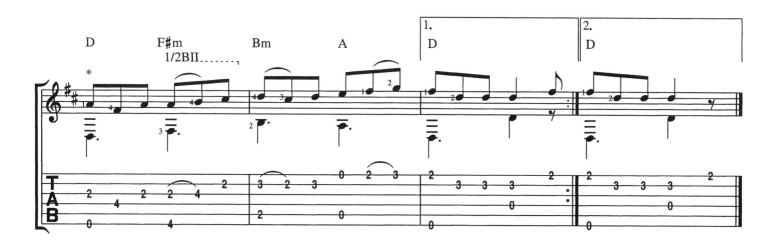

*Alternate fingering

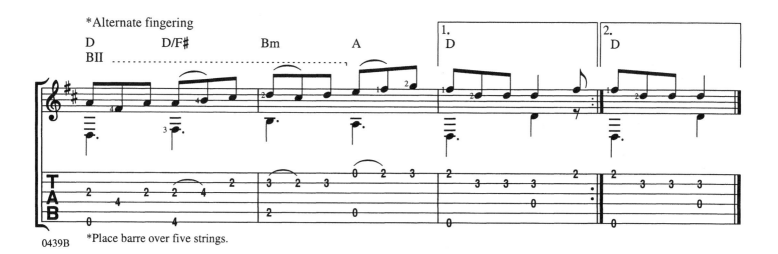

0439B *Place barre over five strings.

paddy whack

Traditional Irish
Arr. G. Weiser

I was told that the title of this tune refers to the Irish pastime of barroom brawling. The first part reminds me of the folk song "Betsy From Pike." It's in *O Neill's Music of Ireland*.

♩. = 104

smash the windows

Traditional Irish
Arr. G. Weiser

The title of this jolly tune could refer to firefighting tactics. It's also known as "The Roaring Jelly."

⑥ = D

♩. = 116

0439B

Hornpipes

BRYNE'S HORNPIPE

Traditional Irish
Arr. G. Weiser

I first heard this tune played by Roy Wall of the Broken String Band on the tinwhistle, and subsequently found it in *O'Neill's Music of Ireland*.

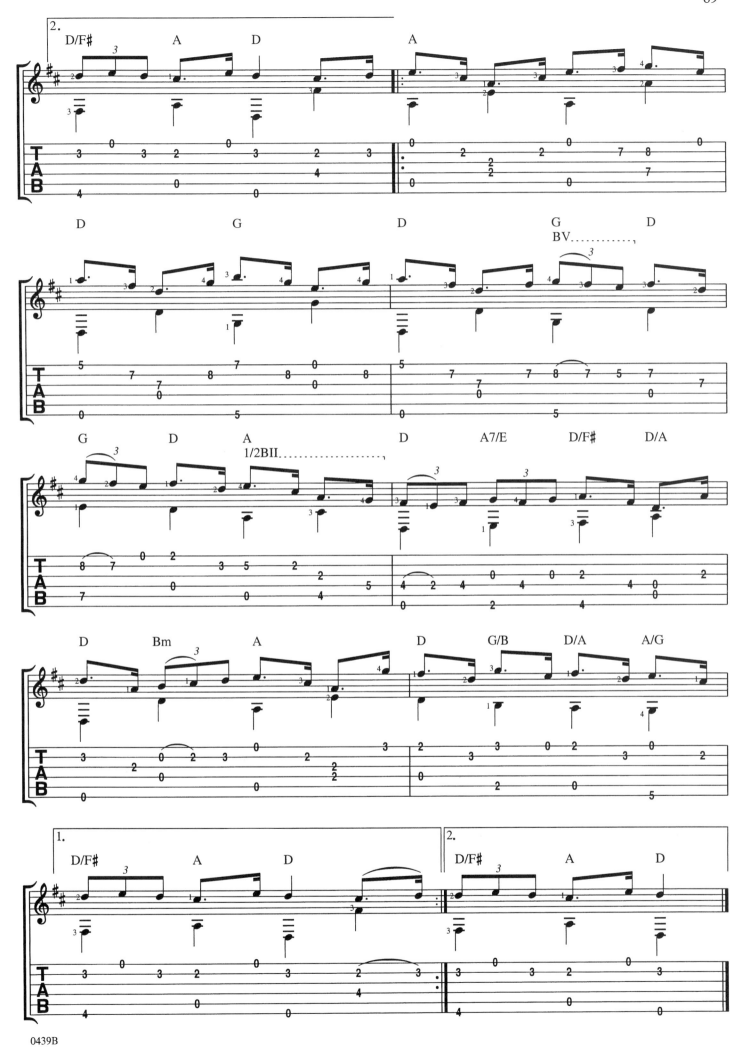

CHIEF O'NEILL'S FAVORITE

Traditional Irish
Arr. G. Weiser

This tune was played by the fiddler Tobin for Francis O'Neill when the latter was compiling his celebrated collection of tunes. Although Tobin knew that the tune was from the Galway area of Ireland, he didn't know the title, so it was dubbed "Chief O'Neill's Favorite." It can also be found in *The Roche Collection* under the title "The Flowers of Adrigoyle."

71

0439B

the cuckoo's Nest

Traditional Irish
Arr. G. Weiser

This one must be quite old, as it can be found in *The Bunting Collection* (1792), and also occurs in numerous variations, which is usually a sign of a tune's antiquity. The version here is based on a setting I heard played by flatpicking great Norman Blake.

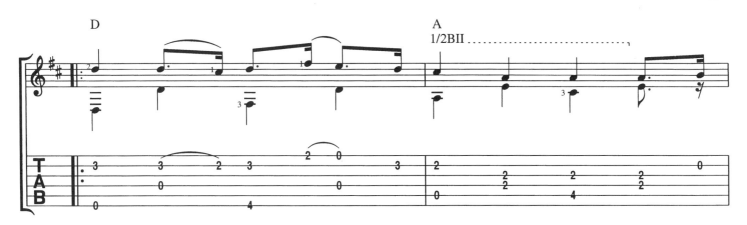

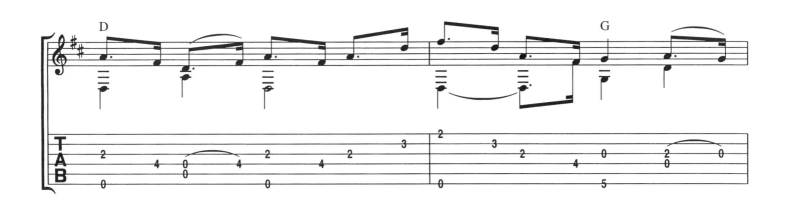

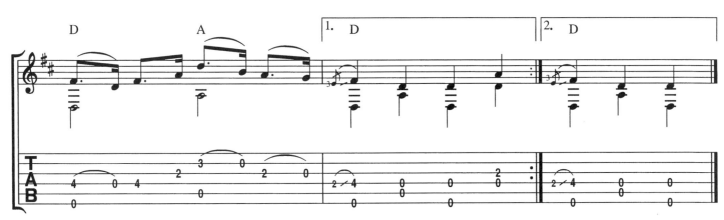

0439B

murphy's hornpipe

Traditional Irish
Arr. G. Weiser

I found this spritely hornpipe in *O'Neill's*.

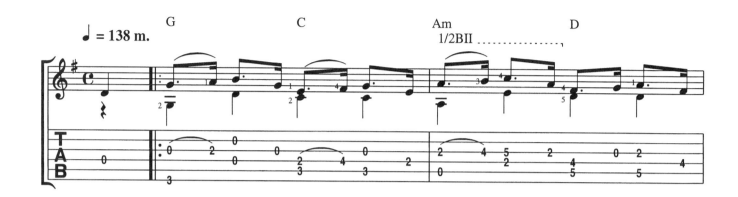

0439B

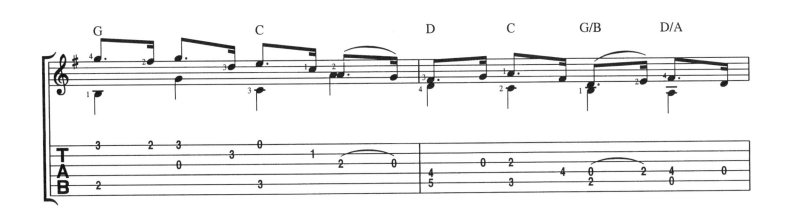

0439B

RICKETT'S HORNPIPE

Traditional Irish
Arr. G. Weiser

This was composed by S.W. Rickett, who ran the country's first travelling circus. Rickett would dance a hornpipe to this tune while standing on top of a galloping horse.

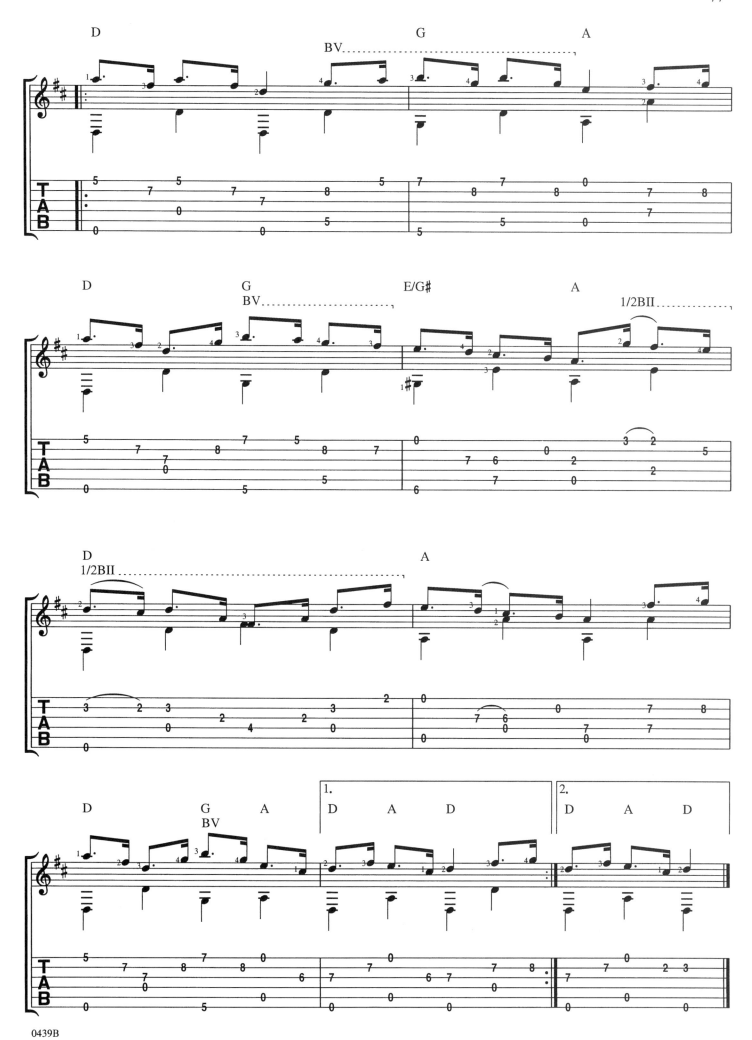

THE TAILOR'S TWIST

Traditional Irish
Arr. G. Weiser

I first heard clawhammer banjoist Ken Perlman play this tune. Said to have been composed by the piper Paddy Taylor, it is also called "Taylor's Twist." The unusual melodic figure in the first measure is the twist in question.

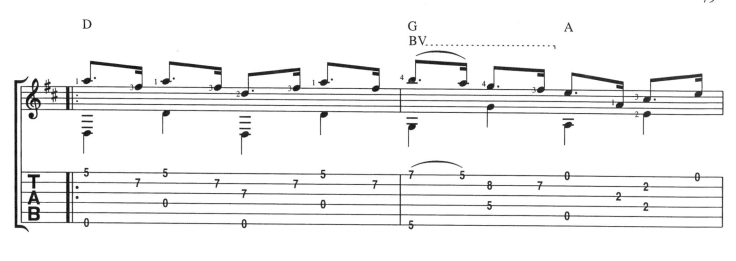

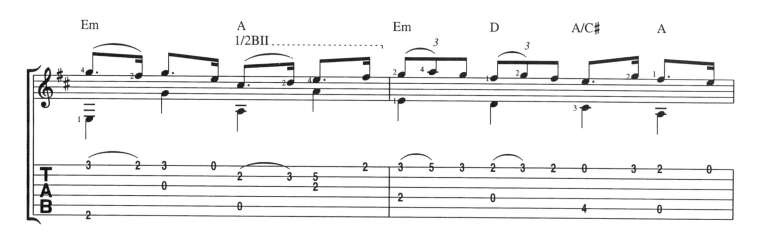

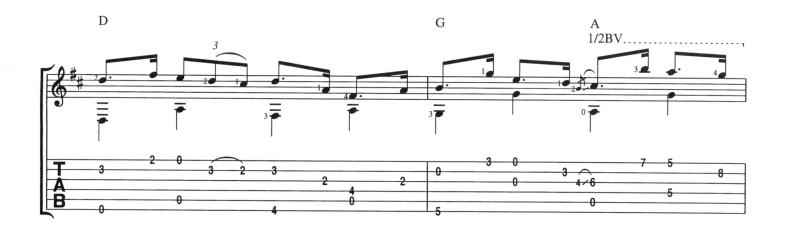

0439B

About the Author

Glenn Weiser was born in 1952 in Ridgewood, New Jersey, and began playing guitar at the age of 13. While in high school, he studied classical guitar with Paul Battat, who was a student of Andres Segovia's pupil Rodrigo Rierez. Later, he studied steel string fingerpicking with ragtime guitarist Eric Schoenberg and also took up harmonica, banjo, and mandolin.

Glenn is the author of several books for guitar and harmonica, his most recent being *The Celtic Encyclopedia: Fingerstyle Guitar Edition*. He has also written for the magazines *Acoustic Guitar, Sing Out!,* and *Acoustic Musician*. Glenn currently teaches guitar in the Albany, New York area and performs in the Northeast.